The Micro World of
ANIMAL AND PLANT CELLS

by Precious McKenzie

Published by Capstone Press, an imprint of Capstone
1710 Roe Crest Drive, North Mankato, Minnesota 56003
capstonepub.com

Copyright © 2022 by Capstone. All rights reserved. No part of this publication may be
reproduced in whole or in part, or stored in a retrieval system, or transmitted in any form
or by any means, electronic, mechanical, photocopying, recording, or otherwise, without
written permission of the publisher.

Library of Congress Cataloging-in-Publication Data is available on the Library of Congress
website
ISBN: 9781663976864 (hardcover)
ISBN: 9781666320923 (paperback)
ISBN: 9781666320930 (ebook PDF)

Summary: All living things are made up of cells. Cells are amazingly small. You can see
them only with a microscope. Discover the parts of cells, how they work, and what the
differences are between animal and plant cells.

Editorial Credits
Editor: Arnold Ringstad; Designer: Sarah Taplin; Production Specialists: Joshua Olson and
Laura Manthe

Content Consultant
Melody Danley, Senior Lecturer, Biology, University of Kentucky College of Arts
and Sciences

Image Credits
Getty Images: wir0man, 17; Science Source, bottom right 27, MedImage, bottom (inset) 8,
Pasieka, bottom (inset) 17, POWER AND SYRED, LIBRERIA BARDON, 27; Shutterstock:
3d_man, 15, Aldona Griskeviciene, middle right 19, BioFoto, top 11, Christoph Burgstedt,
13, bottom left 19, cigdem, Cover, Crevis, 14, DC Studio, 29, Design_Cells, 21, Dmitry
Rukhlenko, 5, Fedorov Oleksiy, 7, Ihor Hvozdetskyi, top (spread) 24-25, Kateryna Kon, top
left 19, Lukiyanova Natalia frenta, 23, Peter Hermes Furian, bottom 11, Sergey Novikov, 8

All internet sites appearing in back matter were available and accurate
when this book was sent to press.

Printed and bound in the United States of America. PO4608

TABLE OF CONTENTS

Words in **bold** are in the glossary.

THE BUILDING BLOCKS OF LIFE

Earth is full of life. Some animals soar across the sky. Others run across the ground or swim through the ocean. Plants sprout out of the ground in sandy deserts and damp rain forests.

There are millions of types of animals and plants. They differ from each other in many ways. But they all have something in common. They are made up of **cells**.

Cells are the tiniest building blocks of life. Most are too small to see without a microscope. Animals and plants are made of many cells. For example, a human being contains around 30 trillion cells. That's a three followed by 13 zeroes!

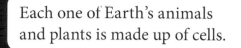

Each one of Earth's animals and plants is made up of cells.

Each cell is a self-contained living thing. It processes energy to stay alive. It creates many of the **molecules** it needs to function. It reproduces, making new cells.

At the same time, cells work together. A complex living thing needs many kinds of cells to survive. Each kind of cell has its own jobs to do.

For example, red blood cells are found in blood vessels. They carry oxygen in the bloodstream. Neurons are found in the brain. These cells send signals throughout the body. **Photosynthetic** cells help plants absorb sunlight.

STEM CELLS

Some cells inside the body are known as stem cells. These cells are able to turn into any other kind of cell. For example, a stem cell might become a blood cell, a nerve cell, or a bone cell. Scientists are closely studying stem cells. Their ability to change into other kinds of cells can be useful in treating diseases.

The red blood cells of mammals are usually shaped like discs.

Muscle cells make it possible for our bodies to move.

Groups of similar cells form tissues. Collections of tissues form organs. Organs work together in organ systems. And a set of organ systems makes up the overall **organism**.

Think about a muscle cell. This type of cell is able to **contract**. Groups of muscle cells form muscle tissue. When they contract, they move bones and other body parts. Some of the body's muscle tissue is in an organ called the heart. The muscle tissue's movement pumps blood out of the heart.

The heart and the blood vessels make up the circulatory system. This organ system moves blood throughout the body. This is necessary for the organism to live. Cells working together make all of this possible.

THE STRUCTURE OF A CELL

Cells often have differences in their structures based on their jobs. For example, red blood cells are small and flexible. This lets them move easily through blood vessels. Nerve cells have long fibers that help them send signals.

Most cells have some parts in common too. Cells have an outer covering. In animal cells, this is a plasma membrane. It protects the cell while also allowing substances in and out. Plant cells have plasma membranes too. But they also have an extra layer of protection. They have cell walls. Cell walls have many jobs, including giving the plant stiffness and strength.

Both animal and plant cells contain cytosol. This is a jelly-like substance. It fills the space between the cells' parts.

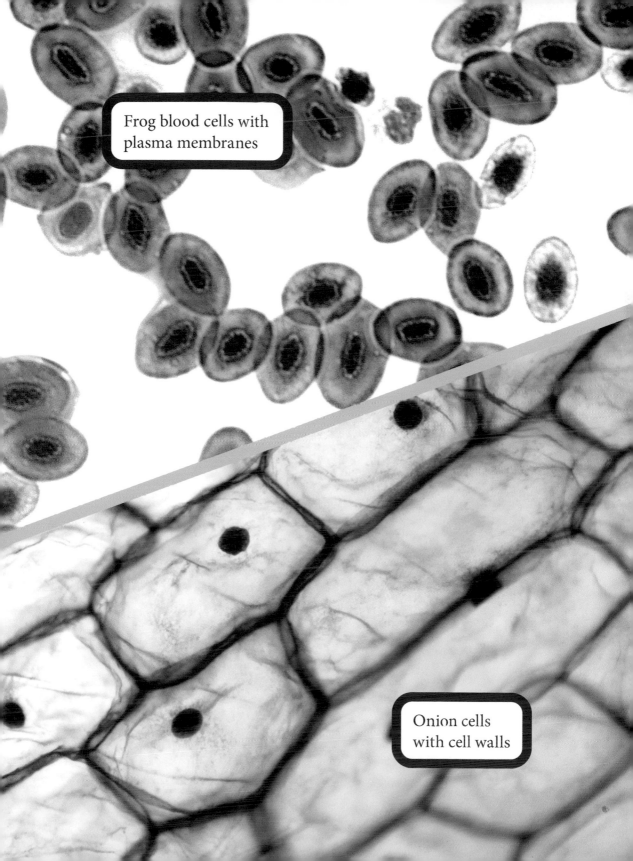

Frog blood cells with plasma membranes

Onion cells with cell walls

Each cell has many different parts. These parts are called **organelles**. The cell's organelles each have their own jobs.

One of a cell's key organelles is the nucleus. It contains **DNA**. The DNA molecule is shaped like a twisting ladder. It contains instructions called **genes**. Genes tell cells which proteins to make.

FACT

Human DNA contains about 30,000 genes. The rice plant's DNA has about 51,000 genes!

Proteins are substances that control many of the organism's traits. For example, a person's genes affect their eye color and height. These traits are passed down from parents to offspring through DNA. Most of an organism's cells have a complete set of the organism's DNA.

A cutaway of the nucleus (center, in red) shows the DNA inside.

Mitochondria have folded membranes within them.

Cells need energy to function. In animal cells, mitochondria are the organelles that handle this. Mitochondria turn nutrients from food into a chemical called ATP. ATP carries energy between parts of the cell.

Plant cells have mitochondria too. But they also have chloroplasts. These organelles carry out a process called photosynthesis. This lets the plant make its own food.

In photosynthesis, the plant takes in energy from sunlight. It uses this energy to turn water and carbon dioxide gas into sugar. Then the plant cells can use the sugar for energy.

Inside chloroplasts are stacks of flat, disc-shaped structures.

The endoplasmic reticulum (ER) is an organelle that produces substances for cells. It is located near the nucleus. There are two types of ER: smooth and rough.

The smooth ER looks like a collection of tubes. The rough ER looks like a group of flat disks stacked together. It gets its name from its bumpy appearance. It is covered in organelles called ribosomes.

Ribosomes follow the instructions from DNA to build proteins. Some are attached to the rough ER. Other ribosomes float freely in the cytosol.

COUNTING ORGANELLES

A single cell is small, but it can contain many organelles. Mammal cells can have thousands of mitochondria. They may contain millions of ribosomes!

Each ribosome is made up of two pieces that work together to create proteins.

Another organelle is the Golgi apparatus. It sorts the substances that the cell makes. This organelle is a stack of flattened membranes. Its name comes from the Italian scientist Camillo Golgi. He first described it in 1898.

Vacuoles are organelles used for storage. Animal cells usually contain many little vacuoles. Plant cells contain one huge one.

Lysosomes are organelles that break down substances. They destroy old parts of the cell. They can even help a damaged cell self-destruct!

FACT

Water usually makes up at least 70 percent of a cell's mass. In animals it is mostly in the cytosol. In plants it is mostly in the vacuole.

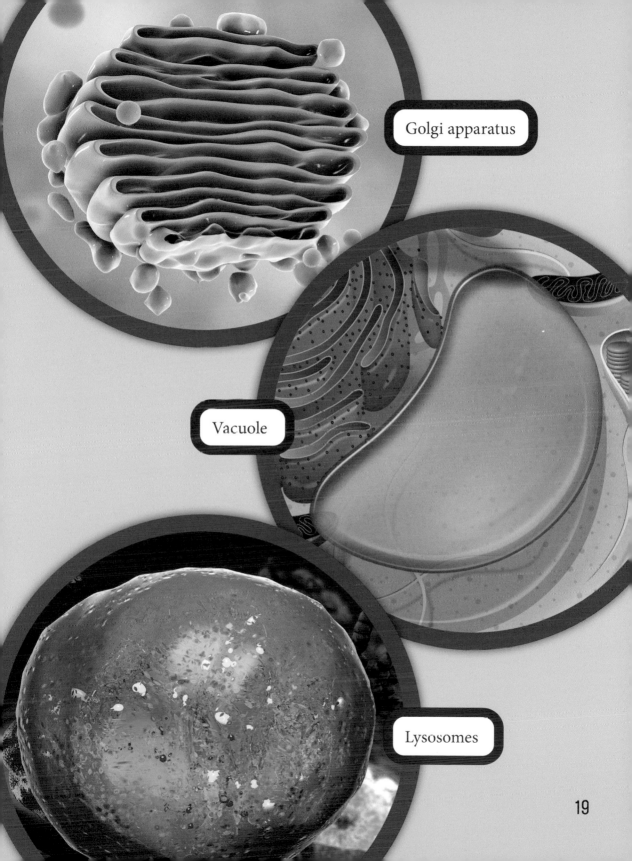

Golgi apparatus

Vacuole

Lysosomes

19

Cells sometimes come under attack from **viruses**. A virus is not alive. It can reproduce only by invading cells.

Viruses attach to a cell's wall or membrane. They break through and enter the cell. Then they use the cell's own parts against it. The cell is forced to make copies of the virus.

Eventually the new viruses break out of the cell. This kills the cell. The new viruses spread to invade more cells. This process makes organisms sick.

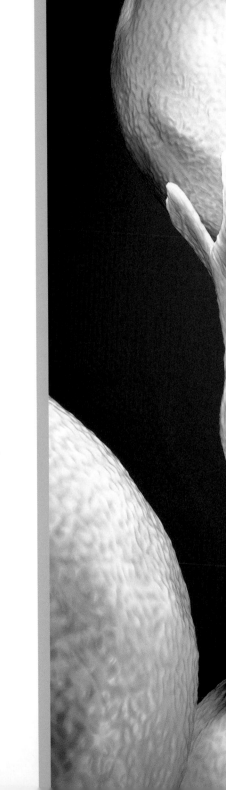

Viruses burst out of a cell after multiplying inside it.

CHAPTER THREE

CELL DIVISION

How are new cells made? Cells go through one of two processes: mitosis or meiosis. Mitosis creates new cells for an organism's body. Meiosis creates cells for reproduction.

In mitosis, the cell first makes a copy of its DNA. The membranes of the nucleus break down. The two sets of DNA move apart. The cell begins to split in half. A new nucleus forms around each set of DNA. Finally, the cell finishes dividing into two new cells. The new cells have the exact same genes as the original cell.

FACT

Some human cells go through mitosis about once every 24 hours. Others never divide at all.

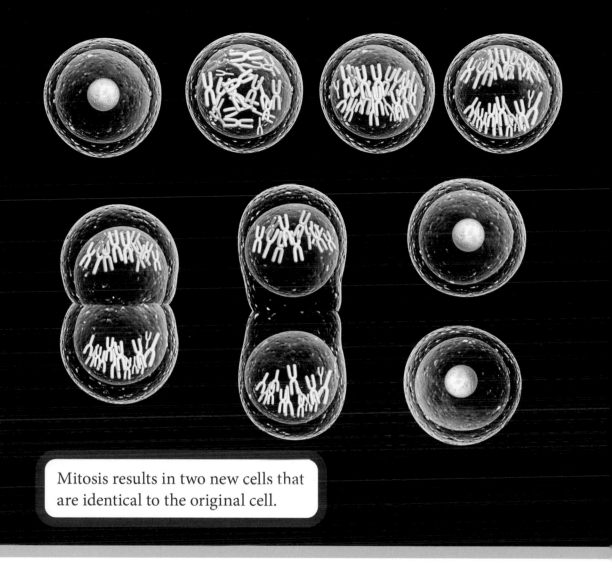

Mitosis results in two new cells that are identical to the original cell.

In animal cells, the area between the two new cells pinches together. This is possible because the cell membrane is flexible. In plant cells, the cell wall is too stiff for this to happen. Instead, a new wall forms in the middle of the cell.

Meiosis is used to make new gametes. These are the cells involved in reproduction.

The stages of meiosis are similar to mitosis. However, the cells divide one more time. That means the result is four cells instead of two. The four new cells each have half the DNA of the original cell.

A yellow powder called pollen contains plant gametes produced by meiosis. Animals such as bees carry it from plant to plant, helping the plants reproduce.

Reproduction happens when a male gamete meets a female gamete. Together, they have a complete set of DNA. They will form a new organism. This new organism has some DNA from its mother and some from its father.

CHAPTER FOUR

STUDYING CELLS

Scientists had to invent microscopes to discover cells. English scientist Robert Hooke designed a microscope in 1665. He used it to look at a piece of plant material called cork.

Under the microscope, Hooke saw that the cork was divided into separate sections. This reminded him of the rooms in **monasteries**. Those rooms were called cells. Hooke called the cork's little sections *cells* too.

Other scientists continued to study cells. Dutch scientist Antonie van Leeuwenhoek made improved microscopes in the 1670s. He saw single-celled organisms, including bacteria. But scientists still had a lot to learn about cells.

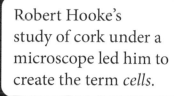

Robert Hooke's study of cork under a microscope led him to create the term *cells*.

Two German scientists made new breakthroughs in the 1800s. Theodore Schwann studied animal cells. Mattias Schleiden studied plant cells. They described the similarities and differences. They said that cells were the building blocks of both plants and animals.

Another German scientist, Rudolf Virchow, also studied cells. In 1855, he described another important idea about cells. This was that all cells are made by other cells. They don't grow on their own from other materials.

Better technology has led to more discoveries. In the 1900s, scientists unlocked the mysteries of DNA. They learned how cells divide and grow. Scientists continue to study the tiny building blocks that make all life possible.

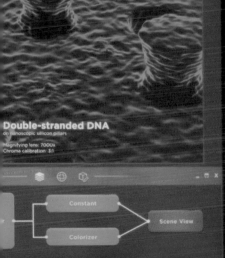

Today's scientists use advanced technology to learn more about cells and how they work.

GLOSSARY

cell (SELL)—a basic building block that makes up a living thing

contract (con-TRAKT)—to produce a pulling force or movement

DNA (dee-en-A)—short for deoxyribonucleic acid, the molecule inside a living thing that includes instructions for that living thing's traits

gene (JEEN)—an individual instruction found in an organism's DNA

molecule (MAHL-uh-kyool)—two or more atoms joined together into a single unit

monastery (MON-uh-stair-ee)—a place where monks, who are members of a religious community, live and work

organelle (or-guh-NELL)—a part of a cell that carries out a job to keep the cell alive

organism (OR-guh-niz-uhm)—a living thing

photosynthetic (foh-toh-sin-THEH-tik)—related to photosynthesis, the process a plant uses to create food for itself

virus (VYE-ruhss)—a tiny nonliving object that invades cells to reproduce, often making the organism sick

READ MORE

Anders, Mason. *Animal Cells*. North Mankato, MN:
Capstone, 2018.

Anders, Mason. *Plant Cells*. North Mankato, MN:
Capstone, 2018.

Huddleston, Emma. *Looking Inside the Human Body*.
Mankato, MN: The Child's World, 2020.

INTERNET SITES

Britannica Kids: Cell
kids.britannica.com/kids/article/cell/352933

DK Find Out!: The Cell
dkfindout.com/us/human-body/your-amazing-body/cell/

National Geographic: Cell Explorers
nationalgeographic.org/interactive/cell-explorers/

INDEX

ABOUT THE AUTHOR

Precious McKenzie is the author of more than 30 books for children. Many of her books focus on animals and nature. She teaches English at a college in Montana. She is also a proud pet-parent to a flock of hens, three dogs, and three cats.